ISBN 978-0-484-41504-0
PIBN 10757551

# CONTENTS.

# THE DEVOUT LOVER.

It is not mine to sing the stately grace,
The great soul beaming in my lady's face,—
To write no sounding odes to me is given,
Wherein her eyes outshine the stars in heaven ;
Not mine in flowing melodies to tell
The thousand beauties that I know so well ;
Not mine to serenade her every tress,
To sit and sigh my love in idleness ;—

But mine it is to follow in her train,

Do her behests in pleasure or in pain,

Burn at her altar Love's sweet frankincense,

And worship her in distant reverence.

## Σῶστρα.

Myself you bid myself to brand
    If I my vow repeal,
And with my own unworthy hand
    My own death doom to seal.


A noteless nothing in a strife
    Where I must win at last,
For I have staked a dearer life
    By far upon the cast.

How dear that life, how high the quest
    That you to me have given,
Unknown to you on earth may rest,
    But may be known in Heaven.

Yet, selfish, I would bend my will,
    Even in its newer birth,
Here to compel your presence still
    To guide my ways on earth.

I know your selfless soul and mind
    Would watch me from above,
Yet, count the wish not all unkind,
    I covet here your love.

Not mine as yet to reach the height
    Where constantly you dwell;
But mine to reverence the light
    That pierced the clouds of hell.

A hell self-made by debt unpaid,

    Wherefrom I might not stir,

But that you came to save my shame,

    The Master's Messenger.

Now if I fail I have lost all,

    But so high placed the prize,

That I perforce must never fall,

    But must with you arise,

To that one Heaven we have on earth,

    A love so far divine,

That it may grow to stainless worth

    And join my soul to thine.

# COME !

Come to me when the earth is fair

With all the freshness of the spring,

When life fills all the liquid air,

And when the woods with music ring ;

When all the wakening flowers rejoice,

And birds remind me of your voice ;

Come to me when the summer's heat

Is strong the breeze of spring to kill ;

When gardens are with perfume sweet,

And when the languid noon is still ;

Come when the opened buds disclose

The glory of the full-blown rose ;

Come to me when the summer fades,

When all the rose's sweets are dead,

When autumn robes the saddening glades,

When purple heather turns to red ;

Come to me when the wrinkled leaf

Falls like the tear of constant grief.

Come most of all when warmth is lost,

When autumn to stern winter yields ;

Come when the bitter edge of frost

Nips all the verdure of the fields ;

Come when all else is dark and drear,

Thy presence then is doubly dear !

# FATHER FRANCIS.

" I come your sin-rid souls to shrive—
Is this the way wherein ye live ? "
  We lightly think of virtue,
  Enjoyment cannot hurt you.

" Ye love. Hear then of chivalry.
Of gallant truth and constancy."
  We find new loves the meetest,
  And stolen kisses sweetest.

" Voices ye have. Then should ye sing
In praise of heaven's mighty king."
  We deem it is our duty
  To chant our darlings' beauty.

" Strait are the gates of worldly pleasure;
The joy beyond no soul can measure."
 Alas ! we are but mortal,
 And much prefer the portal.


" Nay, sons : then must I leave ye so;
But lost will be your souls, I trow."
 Nay, Father, make you merry;
 Come, drawer, bring some sherry.


" Me drink?   Old birds are not unwary—
Still less—Ha—well—'tis fine canary."
 Mark how his old blood prances—
 A stoup for Father Francis !


" Your wine, my sons, is wondrous good,
And hath been long time in the wood."
 Mark how his old eye dances—
 More wine for Father Francis !

" A man, my sons—a man, I say

Might well drink here till judgment-day."

Now for soft words and glances—

But where is Father Francis?


" Heed me, my sons, I pray, no more;

I always sleep upon the floor."

Alas! for old wine's chances,

A shutter for Father Francis!

# MEMORY.

## I.

All down the river's stretch I float,
    While song-birds carol in the air ;
Soft ripples swirl about my boat,
    And all the wakening world is fair.

The world is fair : I should be glad
    When Nature showers her gifts on me ;
Ah me ! my portion is the sad
    Sweet bitterness of memory.

And all my world is in one face,

    One face upon the distant shore,

That looks and longs for me, whose place

    Is with the live who live no more.


For surely this is death in life,

    To know that I can never move

The fates, and that no toil or strife

    Can ever win me her I love.


I hear the loud cicalas sing

    Upon the river's grassy slope,

And still their ceaseless chirrups ring

    Two weary words, " No hope—no hope !"


O fond white arms that loved to play

    About my neck and soothe my pain,

Will there be never more a day

    For me to know your touch again ?

O soft low voice that loved to tell
　Sweet tales to my enraptured ears—
O voice that answered mine so well,
　In laughter and in loving tears !


O love, my lost, my only love,
　Who make the barren years so slow !
I see you in the skies above,
　And in the whirling stream below


Where all the ripples sound and swell
　With all the words you spoke to me,
Till life once more runs fair and well,
　While 1 am fooled by memory.


Come back, O love, to speak one word—
　One little word before I die,—
One of the myriad I have heard
　And still shall hear in memory.

It may not be.   The visions wane
And pale before reality !
The world is cold and dead again —
No joy is left in memory !


Yet could I only this believe,
That one day in the heaven they dream
We two could meet, I'd cease to grieve,
The heavy time would lighter seem.


Naught see I but this greedy world,
A shore whereon the fierce wind drives
Wild wrecks upon the shingle hurled,
The jetsam of divided lives.


What hard and aching punishment
The awful fates contrive for men !
They will not let me give, content,
All days of now for one of then.

And so, where'er I pass my years,

    That darken on the deathward slope,

Those words will echo in my ears,

    Those weary words, " No hope—no hope ! "


## II.

Still cradled on the waters clear—

    The mirror of the dropping sun—

I slowly float, and strangely dear

    Appear the days that now are done.

The sunset breezes lightly kiss

    The tree-tops with their last low breath ;

An' there is happiness in this,

    The happiness that comes with death.

They tower in the waning light

    Those shadowy trees that stud the dell,

And through the softly opening night

    Peals far away the evening bell.

The birds have hushed their noise above,

 Through the long day they sang their best;

They interchange last notes of love,

 And sink with all the world to rest.


A strange and softly solemn mirth

 Is waiting on the dying day:

Peace holds secure upon the earth

 And in my weary heart her sway.


As like a worn-out child I lie,

 To slumber rocked on Nature's breast,

The slow night-wind comes sighing by

 With faintly whispered words of rest.

# RIZZIO TO MARY STUART.

## I.

### *Serenade.*

Lady, lady of my thought,
 See I kneel before thee,
Count my love and service naught,
 Still I must adore thee.

Queen, my Queen, look down on me,
 Far, so far above me;
Put this martyr's crown on me,
 *She can never love me.*

Mary, dear one, were it mine

These bonds to sever,

I would rather stay and pine,

Thy servant ever.


## II.


*Chorus.*


*With mandolin accompaniment.*


Let our song be bright and gay,

Care and grief have naught to say,

All the world is fair as May

For our Lady Queen to-day !


Think no more of what has been :

Sunlight dances on the green,

Never Holyrood has seen

Day more fit for such a Queen !

# A QUESTION.

But is it there the Heaven you sing?

    Shall God make whole the rents of life?

And shall our ears no longer ring

    With the old clang of toil and strife?

Shall things be fair, but never fleet?

    Shall laughter be the voice of mirth?

Shall Nature's face be soft, and sweet

    With tender memories of earth?

Or, while our friends and lovers weep

    That we have passed Death's iron gate,

Shall we be lost in endless sleep,

    Nor dream of those who mourn our fate?

# AN ANSWER.

You ask me, wondering, why I sing,
  And why my lips in laughter part;
The ripples of my mirth all spring
  From the deep sorrow at my heart.

A smile is easier than the tear
  That serves to keep sad memories green,
And always through what is I hear
  The echoes of what might have been.

# DAYBREAK.

Sing, for the night is dying,

   And through the brightening air

The gold-flecked clouds are flying

   The tidings on to bear !

Sing, for the morn is breaking;

   Sing, for the night is done,

And all the birds are waking

   To greet the rising sun.

Sing, for the sun has risen,

   The gloom of night is past,

And we have burst our prison

   And reach the day at last !

## BOAT SONG.

Boat, little boat,

A breeze on thy white sails shall soon light;

Float, lightly float,

Far away into the moonlight—

Winging thy flight,

From the noise and the jar of the world,

In a dream of delight

Shall thy glistening sails be unfurled:

Float far away,

From the glare of the sun's blinding light,

From the heat of the day,

To the cool of the slumbering night:

Float through the bay,

Through the soft ripples' infinite motion;

Bear me away

To the tireless waves of the ocean:

Float to the deep,

To the ocean-bird's long-rolling pillows,

So let me sleep

On a soft-tossing cradle of billows!

## "MOUSSIRENDER RHEINWEIN."

Pour out the bright nectar,

To lay the grim spectre

That lurks in the depths underlying our mirth;

Forget for a minute

That life has aught in it

Save all that is fair on the face of the earth.

Outstrip melancholy,

We'll catch flying folly,

And with her away to her kingdom take wing;

And gay songs and dances

Shall banish our fancies,

That love has a burden or life has a sting.

Our friends Care and Sorrow

May find us to-morrow;

To-night, if they seek us, we'll drown them in

wine,

And all of our troubles

Shall die with the bubbles

That float on the moonlit life-stream of the

Rhine.

## MR. IRVING'S MEPHISTOPHELES.

When the grey shapes of dread, adoring, fall

Before the Red One, towering o'er them all—

The one whose voice and gesture, face and form,

Proclaim him Prince of the unhallowed storm,

Who stands unmoved amid the fiery tide

And rain of flame that tear the mountain side—

Then, as the ribald pageant fades from view,

We think the Fiend himself commands the crew.

But when the mask is down, and when a smile

Wreathes the dark face, and flattering words beguile—

When, whimsical, half careless of deceiving,

He plays upon the student's fond believing;

When from beneath the cavalier's disguise

The Snake unveils the menace of his eyes;

When, with a far-off ring of his despair,

His scathing laughter splits the frighted air—

Then, more than in the Brocken's maddening

revel,

We seem to hear and see the living Devil.

# MISS ELLEN TERRY'S GRETCHEN.

Maid of haviour demure,

All that's sweet and all that's pure;

Girl awakening to love

As to message from above;

Scarcely knowing aught is evil,

Sainthood's horror of the devil;

Misery heaped on Misery,

When the fiend has conquered thee;

Truth of spirit, truth of heart,

Overmastering Satan's art.

When the fatal sword should fall

True to Heaven in spite of all ;

Joy made perfect in a sigh,

Sorrow's very ecstasy ;

Though the Poem's stress and storm

Reach us in an alien form,

Goethe's passion, Goethe's will,

Find we in thy Gretchen still !

# LALAGE.

I could not keep my secret
　　Any longer to myself:
I wrote it in a song-book
　　And laid it on a shelf.

It lay there many an idle day,
　　'Twas covered soon with dust;
I graved it on my sword blade—
　　'Twas eaten by the rust.

I told it to the running brook,
　　With many a lover's notion;
The gay waves laughed it down the stream
　　And flung it in the ocean.

I told it to the zephyr then ;

He breathed it through the morning ;

The light leaves rustled in the breeze,

My fond romances scorning.


I told it to the raven sage,

He croaked it to the starling ;

I told it to the nightingale,

She sang it to my darling.

# BARCAROLLE.

Lady mine,

'Tis thy lover who calls on thy name;

Lady mine,

With the sunset the water's aflame;

There's no guard to keep watch on the gate,

For thee doth my gondola wait;

Let us float with the tide to the deep,

On a cradle of waves shalt thou sleep.

Come away,

For the sunset is dying apace;

Come away,

For here by my side is thy place!

As we float,

And the twilight grows ever more grey,

As we float

'Mid the beautiful death of the day,—

There's a light that I see in thine eyes,

Like the light of the morn that shall rise,

When safely all danger we've passed,

And I call thee mine own one at last.

Row apace,

For the moonlight shines faint on the tide;

Row apace,

For the morning must break on my bride!

## To F. S. W.

Across the vast of ocean, on the shore
That claims you for her own by right of birth,
Receive this echo from the older earth
Which by the right of friendship claims you more;
And by remembrance deep in the heart's core
Of those you parted from but now, of worth
Whose new removal makes us feel a dearth
Whereof we had not prescience before ;
Yet whose insistence does but grow more strong,
And but the more enduring as the days
Follow each other, and their spaces lend
New joy to our glad meeting in the throng
Of hurrying men, new light to the Fate's ways,
That of a passing stranger made a friend.

## To E. J. P.

*On revient toujours a ses premiers amours.*

It is not so, the first we ne'er forget,
And all its thoughts and words unite to mark
The heart's first waking, and the sudden spark
Which fires the train of passion, laid to set
The soul aflame with gladness or regret:
To tune the voice to pæans of the lark,
To song that may dissolve all joys that cark,
Or to the strain " I would we ne'er had met."
Yet when in after years a passing wrack
Has for a space obscured, not the true sun,
But my weak sight, if for a time I rove
With vainer fancies, then I hie me back,
The folly ended almost ere begun,
Not to my first, but to my truest love.

# BELOW THE HEIGHTS.

I sat at Berne, and watched the chain
    Of icy peaks and passes,
That towered like gods above the plain,
    In stern majestic masses;

I waited till the evening light
    Upon their heads descended;
They caught it on their glittering height,
    And held it there suspended:

I saw the red spread o'er the white—
    How like a maiden's blushing—
Till all were hid in rosy light,
    That seemed from heaven rushing:

The dead white snow was flushed with life,

    As if a new Pygmalion

Had sought to find himself a wife

    In stones that saw Deucalion.

Too soon the light began to wane—

    It lingered soft and tender—

And the snow-giants sank again

    Into their cold dead splendour.

And as I watched the last faint glow,

    I turned as pale as they did,

And sighed to think that on the snow

    The rose so quickly faded.

# A CONQUEST.

I found him openly wearing her token;

I knew that her troth could never be broken;

I laid my hand on the hilt of my sword,

He did the same, and he spoke no word;

I faced him with his villainy;

He laughed, and said, "She gave it me."

We searched for seconds, they soon were found;

They measured our swords; they measured the
     ground:

They held to the deadly work too fast;

They thought to gain our place at last.

We fought in the sheen of a wintry wood,

The fair white snow was red with his blood;

But his was the victory, for, as he died,

He swore by the rood that he had not lied.

# A BOUQUET.

I brought my love at eve a mass of flowers

That I had sought throughout the morning
hours:

Brought all that I could find of bright and
sweet,

And trembling laid them down before her feet.


She passed the tulip's pride, the rose's glow,

To choose a bud that scarcely dared to blow;

And said, with kindness gleaming in her eyes,

" I take the flower that others will despise."

# THE IDOL.

ɟ have known it young, I have known it old,

ɟ have found an idol of purest gold ;

And yet there has always come a day

When I saw that the idol's feet were clay.

Of purest gold was fashioned the rest,

In that one idol I loved the best ;

And, ah ! that there should be this to say,

That the feet were clay, the feet were clay !

You may watch till watching outdoes your might,

Never the gold is a whit less bright ;

The idol never shall lose a ray,

But the feet are clay, the feet are clay !

I had counted, half-knowing, the cost before;

" If only the idol is mine to adore,"

I cried, " it is naught if the trumpets bray

That the feet are clay, the feet are clay!


" If the thunder's voice should bear it afar

That the idol is what all idols are;

If I take them for gold what matters it, pray,

If the feet of the idol are only clay?"


And yet the word one day must come

With tune of harp or rattle of drum,

At the birth or the death of a coming day,

That the feet after all are nothing but clay.


Let the people tell it, and let them repeat

What tales they like of the idol's feet:

To this assurance my life I'll hold,

That the idol's heart is of purest gold.

A worshipper must be brave and wise—

The gold is a dauntless gazer's prize;

'Tis the blind who chant in the same dull way

That the feet of our idols are always clay.


Let the darkened eyes of the blind awake,

Let them see the truth for the truth's own sake;

They shall know 'tis a foolish tale is told,

That even the feet are of aught but gold.


Let the blind but open their eyes to the light,—

Nay, let them see truth in their visions of night,—

So may they an idol fashioned behold,

Through and through of the purest gold.

# A RUINED LIBRARY.

" Imperious Cæsar, dead and turned to clay,

Might stop a hole to keep the wind away;"

Here the live thoughts of buried Cæsar's brain

Have served a lazy slut to lay the train

That lights a dunce's fire.   Here Homer's seen

All torn or crumpled in the pettish spleen

Of a spoilt urchin.   Here a leaf from Glanvil

Is reft to mark a place in " On the Anvil; "

Here, too, a heavy-blotted Shakespere's page

Holds up an inky mirror to the age;

Here looking round you're but too sure to see a

Heart-breaking wreck from the " Via Jacobæa;"

Here some rare pamphlet, long a-missing, lurks

In an odd volume of "Lord Bacon's Works;"

Here you may find a Stillingfleet or Blair

Usurp the binding of a lost Voltaire;

And here a tattered Boyle doth gape ungently

Upon a damp-disfigured " Life of Bentley;"

Here half a Rabelais jostles for position

The quarter of a " Spanish Inquisition;"

Here Young's " Night Thoughts " lie mixed with

    Swinburne's " Ballads "

'Mid scraps of works on Poisons and on Salads;

And here a rent and gilt-edged Sterne doth lack

    a ray

Of sun that falls upon a bulging Thackeray;

Here—But the tale's too sad at length to tell

How a book-heaven's been turned to a book-hell.

# HEINRICH HEINE.

This was a singer, a poet bold,

Compact of Fire and Rainbow Gold:

Compact of Rainbow Gold and of Fire,

Of sorrow and sin and of heart's desire—

Of good and of evil and things unknown,

A merciless poet who cut to the bone.

He sounded the depths of our grief and our glad-
ness,

He laughed at our mirth and he wept at our mad-
ness ;

He knew all the joy of the world, all the strife,

He knew, and he knew not, the meaning of life.

# WAITING.

There is her house.   From the trysting stile

It measures an endless half of a mile;

Where I stand, like the sun through April
    showers,

I can see the glow of her garden flowers.

Which of them all is like my love?

The fairy-like bend of the tall foxglove?

The bright pink's blush of the earth's best blood?

Or the delicate warmth of the rose's bud?

She is not like the pink; not like the rose:

She is not like any one flower that grows;

But the beauty of all that the earth can bear

Is gathered for her alone to wear.

# STORM AND CALM.

The waters raged but yesternight,
  The wild wind raised a shrieking wail,
The clouds drove by in swift affright
  Before the fury of the gale.

To-day the sea lies smooth as glass,
  The storm-fiend's voice is heard no more,
The waves in quiet cadence pass,
  And melt upon the peaceful shore;

The laughing ripple of the wave
  Is like the sunny flowers that grow
Upon the summit of a grave,
  Yet cannot mask the death below.

The glad sea smiles to catch the light,

   A smile that can caress and kill;

For yonder wave, with crest so white,

   Bears a dead face that's whiter still.

# A SONG OF BATTLE.

Love with its sorrows and love with its joys,

Love is for delicate maidens and boys;

Love is for women and love is for men,

When love is over what rests to us then?

          The joy of the battle!

There's a time to make love—there's a time to

      make war,—

When love is hopeless 'tis better by far

To put love aside with a sigh and a laugh,

To gird on the sword and a bumper to quaff

         To the joy of the battle!

# A SKETCH.

The sky is blue and bright above,
The trees have donned their soft green dresses,
   And, prattling out its lazy love,
The river takes the sun's caresses.

The air with sweet spring scents is rife,
And pleasant with the talk of thrushes,
   As, glad with a new sense of life,
The year towards its noonday rushes.

Within a corner of the wood
Where the sun's might comes something fainter,
   And dulled the voices of the flood,
There sit a lady and a painter.

Intent the scene's delight to trace,

He deftly plies his practised fingers,

   With eyes that grow towards her face,—

And most on her his labour lingers.


   And while he works the day glides by,

Until with pink the hill-side flushes,

   And with a half-regretful sigh,

He murmurs, flinging down his brushes,


   *The light that travels down the stream,*

*Or, piercing through an opening slender,*

   *Falls through the leaves with fitful gleam—*

*This light my skill can catch and render.*


   *But, sweet, your eyes give out a light*

*That, though I strive from morn till even,*

   *I never can reflect aright—*

*I paint the earth, and not High Heaven.*

## NOW AND THEN.

The sea below was laughing
   In ever-varying hue ;
The flowers here were quaffing
   Their draught of morning dew.

The waves are grey and roaring,
   That then were blue and still,
And winter's torrents pouring
   Where ran the bubbling rill.

There is no sun remaining
   To flush the deathly snow,
The loud wind's long complaining
   Fills all the air with woe.

In place of winter's sadness,

Full summer's joy would reign,

And flood the world with gladness

Were we two one again.

# RAINDROPS.

When thunderclouds hang black in **May,**
Cool drops refresh the weary day :
To man, in childhood's short-lived grief,
Fast-flowing tears bring sweet relief.

The clouds that come in **winter's** train
Drop snow instead of tender rain,
And duller grief can find no tears
To melt the ice of older years.

## " *Der Sandmann.* "

Eyes with depths of wonder

Strike the soul like thunder;

Eyes with half-veiled glances

Pierce it through like lances;

Eyes of soft entreating

Give the sweetest greeting;

Eyes all folk beguiling

Halt 'twixt tears and smiling;

Eyes of soul-charged gazing

Set the heart a-blazing;

Eyes with yellow lashes

Burn the heart to ashes.

## TO SYLVIA.

My dearest, would my all too failing pen

Had some great master's touch ! Nay, even then

It would lack force to tell the debt I owe

To her whose loving help in weal or woe

Is strong to cheer and save me, who can find

A spell assured to check my wavering mind ;

Whose presence in my hours of black despair

Is like the breath of heaven-scented air

To men who stifle in some murderous den—

Like sunlight piercing through a cloud-palled

glen

Where trees hang dark, and stretch wide-seeking
    arms
To catch the wanderer; and weird alarms
Of voices heard in every little breath
Of sullen air threaten despair and death.
This thing there ever is that makes me see
(And at my worst brings newer life to me),
Beyond the body's death the spirit's birth—
My guardian spirit's presence here on earth.

Ἄνω ποταμῶν ἱερῶν.

I look at you in the passionless pride,

   The stainless trust of your maiden years,

And I wonder how much the dog at your side

   Knows of your delicate hopes and fears.

As wise as he is he scarce can guess

   All that I'd give to take his place,

To hear you those pretty thoughts confess,

   To sit at your side and look in your face.

My little lady, this thing is sure

   That till upwards run the sacred streams,

No folly of mine your heart shall lure,

   No word of mine shall disturb your dreams.

# HEIDELBERG : ON THE TERRACE.

We stood upon the castle's height,
   So full of old romances ;
The moon above shone clear and bright,
   And silvered all our fancies.

The Neckar murmured in its flow,
   The woods with dew were weeping ;
And, lighting up the depths below,
   The quiet town seemed sleeping.

The battlements stood grim and still
   In majesty before us,
And floating faintly up the hill
   We heard a students' chorus.

Inspired by the brimming cup,
  Their words were wildly ringing ;
They sang of love, and I took up
  The burden of their singing.


I spoke to you—in sweet surprise
  A little while you hovered ;
Then, in the depths of those gray eyes,
  Your answer I discovered.


We vowed that while the Neckar's flow
  —How low the words were spoken !—
Ran undisturbed these towers below,
  Our troth should rest unbroken.


Again beneath these walls I stand,
  And here my footsteps linger,
When once I pressed with loving hand
  This token on your finger.

But now the well-loved view I see,

　　Its old enchantment misses,

The evening breeze sighs back to me

　　The shadows of our kisses.


Unwearied still the Neckar flows

　　In the soft summer weather;

But last year's leaves and last year's vows

　　Have fled away together!

## AT HER FEET.

What is this I play?
" *Surely she is fair ?* "
Can I help it, pray,
If my fingers stray
To that same old air?
Yet you loved it once,
As we fancied, dearly:
For my sake, you told me.
Neither then could guess
That so soon you'd hold me
For a new toy merely.

Listen once again

To the music's moans—

Try to feel these pleading

Passionate semitones !

Could my voice but ring

With some strain to move y

Ah, me! I can sing

Only this—*I love you.*

# THREE LIGHTS.

The sun shone warm; the morning breeze
Came laughing through the spreading trees;
There fell a sudden joyous gleam
On two who kissed beside a stream.

The day's decline was fierce and hot;
At sunset on the self-same spot
There waited one whose eyes shone bright
And vengeful in the angry light.

F

Last came the moonlight cold and pale,

And, circled with a cloudy veil,

Showed through the trellis of the wood

A white face floating down the flood.

# WAR SONG.

The prison walls were strong;
But our arms were stronger,
           Aha!

The guard resisted long,—
That guard will fight no longer,
           Aha!

This is our battle cry :
*No more shall tyrants rule us,*
           Aha!

Our throats are parched and dry,
But here is wine to cool us,
           Aha!

# THE TWO GATES.

A dream flew out of the ivory gate

And came to me when the night was late.

My love drew near with the proud sad eyes

And the fathomless look of soft surprise.

I slept in peace through the summer night

As I dreamed of her eyes and their depth of light.


A dream came out from the gate of horn

And flew to me at early morn.

I ran to the stable, I saddled my steed,—

We rushed through the dawn at a headlong speed ;

When I reached my love the sun shone bright,

And I found her dead in the morning light.

# THREE.

Which of the three has the dearest breath—
Love, Life, or Death?
Life is full and free and brave,
And cruel and dark like the ocean wave;
Death is cold and calm and cruel,
And keeps in his head a priceless jewel;
Life can grow from a death-field rife,
But Love is Life!

## A CONTINUATION.

" *When the locks of burnished gold,*

*Lady, shall to silver turn,*"*

When thy cheek is wan and old,

And thine eyes no longer burn

With the brightness that was in them

On the day when first we met,

Even though I never win them,

Lady, I shall love thee yet.

* Thackeray's " Adventures of Philip."

## LOVE SONG.

My will is gone to sleep, dear,
    And only you can wake it;
My heart is in your keep, dear,
    To hold or drop and break it.

One day I hold most dear, sweet,
    The day when first I met you;
One thing to me's most clear, sweet,
    I never can forget you.

Daylight without your eyes, dear,
    For me all brightness misses,
And most in life I prize, dear,
    The memory of your kisses.

# X. OLD COURT, TRINITY.

### A GRADUATE MUSES.

The storm and wind torment the pane,
  The rain-drops make the fountain weary,
The court is wrapped in gloom again,
  And all without is dark and dreary.

I light my dusky meerschaum bowl,
  And bend my head on hands supported,
While in my ears the curfew's toll
  Rings clear although the door is sported.

The eddying smoke-wreaths slowly rise,
   In pleasure half, and half dejection ;
I call the past before my eyes,
   And give myself to recollection.

Then through the whirling rings of smoke
   ' I see my old friends' well-known faces
I hear their pleasant song and joke,
   With them frequent the old loved places.

When shall we meet ?  The smoke cloud parts,
   And through the gap I see a vision
Of joining hands and joyful hearts ;
   And cups that clink in swift collision.

Yes: loves of boy and girl may wane,
   But close-knit friendship will not alter ;
And we shall live to meet again,
   And toast—Tobacco and Sir Walter !

## UN FÂCHEUX.

Chaque jour, dès l'aurore,

Je dis que je t'adore ;

Chaque soir, tout de même,

Je me dis que je t'aime.


Pour mes vœux, belle reine,

Me rendras-tu la häine ?

Ainsi soit ; tout de même,

Je dirai que je t'aime.


Si tu veux me bannir,

Je m'en irai mourir ;

Mais mourant, tout de même

Je chant'rai que je t'aime.

## THE SAME.

*Englished from the French.*

As the matins tell the days

So sing I my lady's praise,

Chant " I love thee " all day long,

Chant it still at evensong.

If my vows, fair Queen of Light,

Bring me naught but thy despite,

Be it so; yet still the same

I shall hymn my lady's name.

Wilt thou cruel bid me flee?

That is doom of death to me :

Then my swan-song this shall be,

*" Losing life, I lose but thee."*

## LA DIVE BOUTEILLE.

Ton mépris, ta froideur,
Ont glacé tout mon cœur ;
Mais avec la bouteille
Ma gaîté se réveille.

Quand je verse son sang,
Qui s'écoule gaîment,
Sa chaleur me console,
Et mon chagrin s'envole.

Son reflet me révèle
Un amour bien fidèle,
Que dans tous tes appas
Je ne trouverais pas.

## THE SAME.

*Englished from the French.*

Your coldness, my beauty, your scorn,

My innermost heartstrings have torn ;

No remedy sweeter I ask

Than is found in this delicate flask.

Its life-blood I joyously spill,

And as bumper on bumper I fill,

If I pause to remember your kisses

'Tis to find 'em less charming than this is.

This mistress is constant and true

(Which can scarcely be boasted of you),

Young love's but a fool to old wine,

So here's to the Bottle Divine !

## CHANSONNETTE.

L'amour fait ici-bas la vie;
   N'oublie pas
Que j'ai trouvé l'amour, ma mie,
   Dans tes doux bras.


Bien d'autres vont jurer peut-être
   T'aimer toujours ;
C'est dans mon cœur que tu fais naître
   Les longs amours.

# THE POET AND THE MUSE.

*ALFRED DE MUSSET'S "NIGHTS."*

*With an original Introduction in Verse.*

DEDICATED TO MUSSET'S GREATEST INTERPRETER,

*DELAUNAY.*

# NOTE.

In the following rendering of Musset's "La Nuit de
Mai," "La Nuit d'Août," and "La Nuit d'Octobre," I
have aimed at a version rather than an accurate
translation of the original. I have found it impossible
to combine the letter and the spirit of the original, and
of the two I have preferred to attempt the spirit. I
have not included the beautiful "Nuit de Décembre,"
because it is cast in a method entirely different from
that of the other three. I am fully conscious of my
temerity in having tried, by means of an original
introduction of my own, to give to the three "Nuits"
a coherence which, when detached from the poet's
other work, they might, without something of the
kind, seem to lack. I judge from my own feeling

G

that those who love and admire Musset's writings as much as I do will be inclined to reproach me for having put the three poems into blank verse, instead of trying to reproduce the exquisite varying metres of the original. I did try to do this, and found that I could, to my own thinking, catch more of the spirit of the original in blank verse, than in attempting to suggest the essentially French metres which Musset handled at will. The inferiority of the one faint echo to the other is my only excuse.

*W. H. P.*

# "*THE POET AND THE MUSE.*"

---

## INTRODUCTION.

### THE POET.

" Once more this chamber, empty now so long !

Three months ago I took my well-loved pen

To sing what seemed to me a newer birth—

The passage to a newer, higher life

Through love's bright portal—Love ! there's no such thing·

Save for one's self.  Had I but earlier known—

Three months ago—'tis something to have learned

That love's a lie.   Why, there's no single thing

Around me but's alive with memories

Of that most foolish and most gracious time

When I believed in love.   Oh for one day,

One hour, of that belief!   'Tis dead and gone:

And all its memories shall die with it.

Here's the last page I wrote.   How I remember

The smile that marked approval of the lines;

And here's the writing that three months ago

I stooped to kiss; and here the mark of tears

I shed, when first I knew that smile was false;

But I have done with tears—tears are for fools!

We who've bought wisdom laugh at love-sick

      dreams.

And yet, so fair a dream I never knew,

Nor shall not know again, as this one was.

There would she sit and listen, while I poured

My whole heart forth in song to do her honour;

Or when my fancy failed me, with these keys

She waked responsive music in my soul,

That hung upon her playing and caught up

Her wandering chords, and from their mystery

Drew out a sure and beautiful intent.

Was I aweary, she would cheer my spirit

With jocund music ; was my brain too full

With crowding images, she struck the note

That stilled the tumult, cleared confusion off,

And left the majesty of ordered thought.

Whose weariness doth thank that music now ?

Let me not think of it !   Easy to say—

Easy as for a lonely shipwrecked wretch

To say, ' I will not think I am alone ; '

Easy as for a watcher by a corse

To say, ' I will not think that this is death.'

My heart is dead, and what shall bring it life ?

Most idle sorrow for an idle thing—

But what shall cure it ?   All that once I loved

Seems barren, and my mind, that did delight

To give expression to the fleeting forms

Of fancy, is weighed down with weariness

Of recollection—all the world is dark,

And I the heaviest blot upon its face.

She, who before I knew that faithless one,

Filled all my life with dreams of happiness,

Of fame and name immortal—she, my Muse,

My comforter, has left me here to die."

Thus bent he helplessly before the storm

Of disappointed hopes, to rise again

To life renewed, and then to sink afresh

To deeper death of spirit;  whence once more

He rose and sang, for sing he must or die—

Now lightsome, now impassioned, now ablaze

With scornful rage at those who sully Art;

Now in the drama's mirror showing forth

Those mighty dames and proud-plumed cavaliers,

Ill-favoured husbands, cross-grained servitors,

Who meet and bow, and talk, and laugh, and weep,

Till cracks the lava-crust beneath their feet,

And the long waiting Fate engulfs its prey.

Thus from his woes he gathered joy for us—

The joy of fancy perfected by art ;

And at his direst need the Muse came down

Three times to cheer him in his solitude.

# A MAY NIGHT.

## THE MUSE.

Take thy lute, Poet.    Turn and kiss thy Muse!

It is the birth-night of the Spring.    The breeze

Stirs with fresh life to catch the new-born scent

Of sweetbriar blossoms ; on the first green boughs

The wagtail perches, waiting for the dawn.

Take thy lute, Poet.    Turn and kiss thy Muse!

## THE POET.

How dark the valley lies !    Methought I saw

A veiled form leave the meadow, and flit forth

Among the trees, and with a lightsome step

Disturb the grass.   It was a fantasy

That dream-like passed and vanished into air.

## THE MUSE.

Take thy lute, Poet.   Night upon the lawn

Rocks in its perfumed veil the zephyr's breath;

The maiden rose shuts on the burnished drone

Drunk with her sweets, and dies upon a kiss.

Silence is lord.   Think, Poet, of thy love.

To-night beneath the lime-trees' darkling arms

The dying sun's farewell is passing sweet;

To-night immortal nature brings again

Her dearest perfumes for the whispered love

That waits upon the bridal of the spring.

## THE POET.

Why beats my heart so fast?   What is this thrill

That terrifies my pulses?   Did I hear

A stranger's knock?   Why does my dying lamp

Blaze into sudden light?   Sweet heaven, help me!

I tremble.  Who is this?  Who calls?  'Tis no one;
And all I hear is the untiring clock
That knells the poorness of my solitude.

### THE MUSE.

Take thy lute, Poet, for the Heaven-sent wine
Of youth runs strong to-night throughout my veins,
And I am fevered, longing still for thee.
When, paling even at my wing's first touch,
Weeping, thou cam'st for comfort to my arms,
'Twas for a bitter wound I gave thee balm;
For love's betrayal had transfixed thy heart,
Too young for such experience; but to-night
'Tis I who come to thee for help.   I pine—
I waste in vainly hoping for thy voice.
If the dawn finds me helpless, I shall die.

### THE POET.

Is it thy voice, sweet Muse, that calls?   Is't thou,
My flower of love immortal, who alone

Lov'st me with faithful love?   It must be so,

For through the midmost depth of night I feel

The spreading glory of thy golden robe,

Whose rays have pierced the darkness of my heart.

### THE MUSE.

Take thy lute, Poet.   'Tis the immortal Muse

Who saw thee sorrowing in the silent night,

And, like a bird who hears her young brood's call,

Came down from heaven's heights to weep with

thee.

Thou art ill at ease.   Some solitary grief—

Some love has come to thee—some earthly love—

Some vain and fleeting shadow of delight.

Raise we a song on high, whose strains shall be

Of thy lost happiness and bygone woes !

Seek we in close embrace a world unknown !

Waking at chance the echoes of thy life,

We'll sing of glory, madness, happiness,

Lost in whatever dream the Fates may send !

Fly to the kingdom of forgetfulness !

We are alone, and all the world is ours.

Here Scotland lies, there Italy's warm sky,

And Greece, my mother, with her honey's sweets.

Tell me what golden dreams our song shall
    cherish—

What tale of sorrow shall compel our tears ?

When thine eyes opened on this morning's light,

What angel scattered lilac on thy couch,

And filled thine ear with murmured tales of love ?

What shall we sing ?   Hope, sadness, or delight ?

The steeled battalions weltering in blood,

The lover's silken ladder, or the foam

That the swift courser scatters down the wind ?

Or shall we hymn the Hand that day and night,

In the unnumbered lamps of Heaven's house,

Lights up the eternal oil of Love and Life ?

Or shall we cry to Tarquin, " It is time ;

The night is here!" or dive to bring to light

The pearl that lies beneath the ocean's deeps?

Or lead the goats to browse beneath the shade

Of the bitter ebony-tree? or show the heavens

In all their graciousness to Melancholy?

Or track the hunter on the mountain steeps?

The hind beseeches him with tearful eyes—

She has left her new-born calf within her lair:

Stooping, he draws the knife across her throat,

And throws the offal to the panting hounds.

Or shall we paint a maid with blushing cheek

Hurrying to mass, a page close at her heels?

She kneels, unheedful, at her mother's side;

Her lips, half-open, have forgot their prayer;

She listens trembling while the echoing aisle

Rings back the clank of some bold gallant's spurs.

Or shall we bid the heroes of old time,

Mounting all armed upon their battlements,

Awake once more what strains the troubadours

Learnt from the deeds that slumber in the past?

Shall we compose some gentle elegy?

Shall he of Waterloo recount his deeds,

And tell how many lives his sword mowed down

Before he felt the stroke of Azrael's wing,

And crossed his hands upon his iron breast?

Or on a satire's gibbet shall we hang

The thrice-sold name of some pale pamphleteer,

Who, hunger-tempted, from his haunts obscure

Came shivering with envy's impotence

To stab at genius and its lofty hopes,

And bite the laurel that his breath had fouled?

Take thy lute—take thy lute, for I must speak.

My wings upbear me on the breath of spring—

The fresh wind wafts me to the higher airs,

One tear from thee—God help me!—it is time!

## THE POET.

My Muse, if all thou askest is a kiss

From lips that love thee, and a tear of mine,

They are thine at once.  Remember thou our loves
When thou fliest heavenwards.   For me, I sing
No more of fame, or hope, or happiness,
Nor even grief can give me food for song.
My lips keep silence, for my heart must speak.

### The Muse.

Think'st thou that I am like an autumn wind
That lightly drinks the tears that fall on tombs,
And looks on sorrow as a water-drop ?¦
Poet, 'tis I who stoop to kiss thy lips !
The weed I would pluck thence is Indolence ;
Thy sorrow rests with God—whate'er may be
Thy young life's burden, let the wound grow wide
With which grief's angels have transfixed thy
        heart.
'Tis by woe's greatness men become most great.
But think not, when grief comes, thou should'st
        be dumb ;

The finest songs are children of despair,

And some immortal strains are one vast sob!

When after weary hours the pelican

Seeks his reed-nest amid the evening mists,

His hungry brood await him on the strand,

Spy him from far, and crowding to their sire

With cries of joy anticipate their prey,

And o'er their monstrous pouches shake their

     beaks.

He with slow gait ascends a rocky point,

Shelters his little ones with drooping wing,

And looks to heaven with a mournful glance.

Blood in long streams flows down his outspread

     breast,

For vainly has he scoured the ocean's depths—

The seas were empty, barren was the shore,

And to his hungering brood he gives his heart.

Sombre and silent, couched upon the stone,

Sharing his very life among his sons,

He lulls his anguish with his love divine.

Watching his life-blood leave him drop by drop,

Drunk with the joy and pain of sacrifice,

He sinks upon his festal bed of death.

Or if he fears his children, satisfied,

May leave him living to a lingering death,

Rising, he stretches to the wind his wings,

Strikes wildly at his heart, and with the blow

Cries to the night so dreadful a farewell

That from the bank the frighted sea-birds flock,

And wanderers benighted on the shore

Know death is near, and make their peace with
      God.

Poet, 'tis thus with great ones of thy race,

They let the crowd that lives a day laugh on,

And feast it as the pelican his brood ;

But when they sing their song of hope betrayed,

Of grief neglected, unrequited love,

The strain is scarce a spur to merriment.

Their lofty eloquence is like the blade

That sweeps a flashing circle through the air,

But ever leaves some blood-drop in its track.

## THE POET.

Insatiate vision ! Muse ! it is too much

Thou dost demand.  Where is the man would
write,

When the north wind is passing, on the sand ?

I have known the time when youth upon my lips

Was ready, bird-like, with a ceaseless song ;

But sorrow tried me with her fiery touch,

And the least word that I could speak of this

Would break my lyre like a shatter'd reed.

# AN AUGUST NIGHT.

## The Muse.

All through the summer's heat, since when the sun

Passed Cancer in the vastness of the heavens,

I know no joy, and silently await

The moment when my loved one's voice shall call.

Empty too long his wonted place has been—

The merest tomb of bygone happiness.

I only come enshrouded in my veil,

As might a widow, weeping, to the tomb

Of a lost child, that I may lay once more

My burning brow on the half-open door.

## The Poet.

Hail, faithful one, my glory and my love !

She is the best and dearest loved of all

Who waits so constantly for him who strays.

The voice of men, and baser voice of greed,

Have torn me for a little from thy side.

Hail, Mother! at whose touch the name of grief

Is blotted.   Open wide thy sheltering arms

To take thy child, for I must sing once more.

## The Muse.

O thirsty heart, worn out and sick with hope,

Why dost thou flee thyself so long, so oft?

What canst thou win for thy return but pain ?

What dost thou while night long I wait for thee?

'Tis a pale lightning in an ink-black night

Thou seek'st ; and in the dregs of worldly lusts

Thou'lt find vain scorn of our untarnished love.

Thy study's bare and empty when I come ;

And while in anxious solitude I wait,

Leaning upon this balcony, and turn

A viewless eye upon yon garden wall,

Thou art blindly following thine evil star.

Some swelling beauty chains thee to her side,

And thou forgett'st all else.   The vervain here

Lies dead ; in happier days its springing shoots

Should have been watered with a poet's tears.

These drooping leaves do but reflect myself.

Sweet one, we both shall die of thy neglect!

The flower's fleeting scent will bird-like mount,

And bear my memory with it to the skies.


### THE POET.


I crossed the fields to-night, and in my path

I marked a flower drooping unto death,

A sweetbriar's sickly blossom.   By its side

A green shoot nodded on the self-same bush,

And bore a new bud bursting into life.

The younger was the fairer.   So it is

With man who ever grows to newer health.

## THE MUSE.

Ah! thou art always man, with streaming tears

And dust-disfigured feet and sweat-dropped brow;

The clang of blood-stained battle fills thine

ears,

And thy heart strives to hide its deadly wound.

Search through the world, and find man's life the

same:

Desires, remorse, hands stretched and inter-

changed—

The same old actors and the same old play—

And let hypocrisy do what it will,

In human life there's nothing true save death.

Dear one, the poet in thee dies, and naught

Wakes into song the dumbness of thy harp.

Thy soul is drowned in an inconstant dream—

Thou know'st not that a woman's love can
    change
And waste to tears the soul's most precious gifts—
Yet tears count dearer in God's sight than blood.

### THE POET.

I crossed the vale, and heard a bird that sang
Upon her nest; her brood had died at night,
And yet she sang to greet the breaking morn.
Then weep not thou, my Muse; when all seems
    lost
We still have hope on earth, and God in heaven.

### THE MUSE.

What wilt thou find the day that misery
Shall drive thee lonely to thy lonely home?
And when thy trembling hands shall wipe the
    dust
From this poor shelter that thou wouldst forget?
How wilt thou dare, returning to thy home,

To ask for welcome and for peacefulness?

All through the day a haunting voice will cry,

" What hast thou done with life and liberty? "

Think'st thou to find at will thy banished self?

The Poet's song is born within his heart:

Call thou to thine—thou'lt find its music dead!

Love will have shattered it, and evil's touch

And passion's scars have turned it into stone;

And for all sign of life in it, thou'lt find

The deadly writhing of a new-killed snake.

Ah! who shall help thee then?   What can I do

When the Almighty shall forbid my love?

When these bright wings, impelled against my
   will,

Bear me to Him to save myself from thee?

Poor child! No danger hung above our loves

When thou didst stray at evening, lost in thought,

'Neath the white poplar and the chestnut's green:

I lured thy heart with innocent wiles to mine,

And wandered with thee through the darkening

> wood.

Then was I young—a nymph; the Dryads peeped

To see me through the crannies of the trees.

What tears were shed then in our wanderings

Fell pure as gold into the crystal streams.

O love, where is that time?  Whose hand hath

> plucked

> ie fruit from off my consecrated tree?

Ah me! that goddess saw thy brilliant youth

Who in her grasp holds human strength and

> health.

Insensate tears have paled thy loveliness.

Thou'lt lose thy beauty and thy better self,

And I who still will love thee with the love

That cannot falter, if the offended gods

Shall pluck thy genius from me—if I fall

From heaven to earth—what wilt thou answer

> me?

### THE POET.

Since the wood-bird can flutter still and sing

Upon the branch that bears her ruined brood;

Since the field-flower, opening to the morn,

Seeing a newer bud burst forth hard by,

Can droop content and die with dying night;

Since in the depths of the green canopy

We hear dead branches crackle in our path;

Since in his course through Nature's vastnesses

Man finds no wisdom but in pressing on,

With memory dead save for each instant step;

Since e'en the hardest rocks drop into dust;

Since to-night's death brings forth to-morrow's

      life;

Since from war's screams and murder's comes

      forth good;

Since the bright herb that gives us bread can grow

Up from the silent horror of the grave—

What's life or death to me, my Muse?  I love,

And will grow pale.  I love, and I will mourn,

And give my genius for one well-bought kiss ;

I love, and I will feel upon my cheek

The everlasting current of love's tears ;

I love, and will sing indolence and joy—

My maddest happiness—my passing griefs ;

Ay, and for ever I would blazon forth

This thing—that having sworn to let love go,

I have sworn again to live and die for love.

O bitter heart!  O heart who thought'st that
      death

Had clasped thee, quit thy wretched garb of
      pride—

Love yet again, and find new life in love.

Be as the flowers, and rise to brighter life :

Thou hast felt grief, and grief must feel again ;

Love thou hast known, and shalt for evermore.

# AN OCTOBER NIGHT.

## THE POET.

The grief that weighed me down has disappeared
And left me like a dream—far off and dim
Its memory seems, like night-engendered mists
That with the dewdrops melt before the dawn.

## THE MUSE.

Tell me, my Poet, what may be this pain
That for so long has kept thee far from me.
Ready to greet the name, the much-loved name
Of comforter, I come to comfort thee.
Grief's grace is wasted in the secrecy

That thou hast given it.   Hadst thou called on me

In thy first days of dark and silent woe,

I had been there to help.   I too have wept,

Knowing thine absence, knowing not its cause.

Tell me what grief it is I catch from thee?

Whence come the tears thine eyes have lent to

    mine?

### THE POET.

Thou wilt call mine the commonest of griefs,

But 'tis man's nature to exalt himself

And think the world's affliction his alone.

### THE MUSE.

It is the common mind that makes grief common;

Let thy heart speak to mine, and gather strength

Sharing its weight of miseries with me.

### THE POET.

I know not by what name to call my grief,

If I must speak of it—whether to count it

For pride, love, madness, or just such a thing

As all men suffer; nor no more can know

If any man can profit by the tale—

But thou shalt hear it; take thy lyre, my Muse,

And let my memory speak to its sweet chords.

### The Muse.

Stay, Poet! ere thou tell me of thy grief

Bethink thee well—is it or not o'erpast?

Remember that, unswayed by love or hate,

Thou must relate the story to thy Muse;

No remnant of the passion that has wrecked thee

Must reach mine ears—unsullied they must be;

The Poet, not the man, must speak to me.

### The Poet.

I am so far recovered from mine ills,

I cannot, when I would, remember them;

Or if they will assault me still, meseems

That they befell some stranger. Fear not then,

Dear Muse: thine inspiration is a shield

That shall keep both of us secure and sound.

'Tis sweet to weep, but double sweet to smile,

Remembering sorrows that we might forget.

### THE MUSE.

E'en as with loving watch a mother bends

Across the cradle of her darling child,

So stoop I trembling to the wakening heart

That slept so long and gave no sign of life.

Speak, dear one, for my lyre's plaintive note

Anticipates thy voice's loved accords,

And the brave sun shines forth to sweep away,

Like a vain dream, the darkness of the past.

### THE POET.

O days of work!   Mine only days of life!

O thrice-dear solitude! praise be to heaven,

Once more my Muse descends to light these walls,

Once more my Muse and I will sing together!

To her I'll bare my heart—she shall know all!

A woman was my tyrant; I her slave,

Who for one glimpse of bliss sold all my youth.

When in the evening's light beside the brook

We walked together on the silvered grass,

When the white spectral aspen marked our path,

And the cloud-haunted moon sent trembling rays

To give us fitful guidance, when these arms—

O God! I see it all! let me forget it!

I guessed not then the goal of all my hopes.

But wrathful Fate must have been poor of prey

When it looked down and fixed its gaze on me,

And plagued me thus for seeking happiness.

## THE MUSE.

The memory's sweet that hangs about thy heart,

'Tis fear that shuns it—let thy courage rise,

And clasp remembrance of that happy time.

From Fate, if it were cruel, take thy cue,

And not in tears, but smiles, enshrine thy love.

## The Poet.

No! Smiles I keep for woe—but I have said it:

Thou, Muse, shalt hear an unimpassioned tale

Of all my weary dreams and bitter madness;

I'll tell the time, the occasion, and the place—

How I remember! 'Twas an autumn night,

Chilled with the solemn rhythm of falling leaves;

The sighing wind, striking the same sad note,

Half lulled the dark forebodings of my spirit.

At an unlighted window, leaning out,

I watched with greedy eyes for her return;

And as I listened, through the silent dark,

There came about my heart an unknown grief

That grew into the monster of suspicion.

The street was sombre—not a soul astir—

Far off, vague human forms passed here and there,

And the wind, happening on some yawning gate,

Dejected, howled, as mocking human sighs.

I know not whence the dreadful presage came

That gave my soul unrest and killed my hope.

She came not; then with hand-supported head,

I swept the view with love-enkindled eyes.

I have not told thee—nor no words can tell—

The madness of the love I bore to her.

But I had rather died ten thousand deaths

Than lived a single day beyond her sight.

So, while this dreadful night dragged out its length,

I strained each nerve to break the heavy chain

That held me captive: called her frail and false,

And counted o'er the wrongs that she had done me.

Then came remembrance of her fatal beauty,

And crushed rebellion even in its birth.

Day broke at last, and found me caught by sleep.

When the sun waked, I waked and looked for her:

I heard her step, I rushed to question her:

" Whence com'st thou ? from whose arms ? whose kisses hang

      kisses hang

About thy lips ? "    What need to tell thee more

Or redeliver all the words that grief,

And wrath, and shame conspired to heap on her?

" Leave me ! " I cried ; " pale spectre of my youth,

Reseek the tomb that should have guarded thee ;

Let me forget the faith I once did hold,

Or, if my memory must bear thee still,

Let me believe I dreamed of such an one."

### The Muse.

Calm thee, my Poet, for thy very words

Have made me shudder.   Oh, my love, thy wound

Is but too ready to re-open still ;

Deep it must be, and this world's miseries

Most slow in their decay.   Forget, my child,

And wipe from out thy memory's records

That woman's name that must not pass my lips.

### The Poet.

Oh, shame on her who taught me truth could die !

Shame on thee, woman of the sombre glance,

Whose fatal love o'ershadows all my youth !—

'Tis thy corrupting gaze has made me curse

The very name and thought of happiness ;

Thy loveliness doth measure my despair,

And, if I even doubt the truth of tears,

Why—I have seen thee weep.   Oh, shame on

     thee !

Thou foundst me simple as a child ; my heart

Opened to thine as flowers do to the sun.

Shame on thee, mother of my earliest grief !

Thine was the spring of tears, that naught may

     check

Until they drown thy loathed memory !


## THE MUSE.


Enough, my Poet !  Faithless she has proved ;

But though her faith had lasted but one day,

Thou shouldst not wrong that one day's memory.

If it o'er tasks the stretch of human strength

To give full pardon to a wanton ill,

Let not thy heart be gnawed by hatred's fangs,

But for forgiveness let oblivion stand.

The dead sleep quietly within the earth,

So should dead love within the human heart.

Think'st thou that heaven's providence can sleep,

Or aim its shafts at chance? This grief of thine,

Opening thy heart, has taught thee how to live.

Man is apprenticed to his master, Sorrow,

And he knows not himself who suffers nothing.

It is a law severe—a law supreme,

Old as the world, and as fatality,

That men must be baptized in suffering.

Tears are the dew that quickens human hearts.

How shouldst thou value life's delights, if thou

Hadst never known the pain that is their price?

How shouldst thou love the garden-scented
      breeze,

The birds' rejoicing anthem, and the arts

That lend a grace to Nature, if through all

Thou didst not hear the echo of past sighs?

The heaven's illimitable harmony,

The silence of the night, the murmuring flood—

How shouldst thou love all these, unless thy pain

Had made thee long for an eternal rest?

What, then, is thy lament?   Immortal hope

Should  spring  in  thee from sorrow.   Wherefore
      hate

Thy young experience, or deplore an ill

From which is born thy better, wiser self?

My child, keep pity for that faithless one

Whose beauty caused thy tears—for she it was

Who showed thee Sorrow's road to happiness.

She loved thee; but the Fates had chosen her

To bring thee face to face with life's intent—

Pity her, for she was their instrument.

Trust me, her tears were true; and were they false,

Pity her still—for thou know'st how to love.

## THE POET.

Thou art right : and hatred is an evil thing,

Whose viperous writhing in our hearts sets up

Infinity of horror.   Hearken, then,

My goddess, and record this solemn vow !

By the blue vault of yonder gracious heaven ;

By the bright sphere that borrows Venus' name,

And pearl-like trembles in the far-off sky ;

By Nature's grandeur and almighty love ;

By the firm star that is the sailor's guide ;

By all the meadows, all the woods and groves ;

By life's omnipotence—ay, by the sap

That doth invigorate the Universe,

I banish thee for ever from my mind—

Wreck of a maddening and insensate love,

Dead memory of a bygone tale of woe !

For thee, who wert my heart's love—my soul's life,

The moment of forgetfulness shall be

The time of pardon—each shall pardon each.

The charm is broken, and with one last tear

I waft thee to the echoes of the past.

Now to our loves, my Muse!   Inspire me straight

As thou wert wont, with some all-joyous song!

See how the flower-laden lawn awakes,

To take the morning; see how startled night

Rolls like a gauze away before the dawn!

We two will rise again to newest life

Beneath the blessing of the sun's first rays!

**THE END.**